D1326137

ARCHIVE COPY

This book is due for return on or before the last date shown
above; it may, subject to the book not being reserved by
another reader, be renewed by personal application, post, or
telephone, quoting this date and details of the book. ♻ 100%
recycled paper.

HAMPSHIRE COUNTY COUNCIL
County Library

SHORT-WALKS
in the
NEW FOREST

by
David Dickens

COUNTRYSIDE BOOKS
3 Catherine Road
Newbury, Berkshire

Previously published by
Inklon Publications

This revised edition 1992

by

Countryside Books

3 Catherine Road, Newbury, Berkshire

ISBN 1 85306 159 X

Editor	**Angus Waycott**
Photography	**Angus Waycott**
	Peter Swatton
	Peter Dickenson
Illustrations	**Ruth Marson**

Produced through MRM Associates Ltd., Reading
Printed by J. W. Arrowsmiths Ltd., Bristol

This book is dedicated to my eighty year old Mother-in-Law who has capriciously survived many of these walks with us against all the odds.

Preface to the Second Edition

Since the first publication of this book, many families of evident 'townies' have been seen, tightly clutching their copies, picking their merry way along these paths in the depths of the Forest. Laughs rise up as Mum mistakes a cow-pat for a piece of firm ground, or Grandad is unceremoniously hoisted over a boggy stretch. This has been my greatest reward, watching children and adults alike delighting in what is obviously a totally new experience to them of walking in the wild. This book was written for people's pleasure and fun; I hope your happy voice may reach my ears on one of these walks one day.

After the great gales of 1988 and 1990 a diminutive figure could be seen removing huge branches of storm-blown trees that blocked the paths of some of these walks. My Mother-in-Law is now past 85. She is as indomitable as ever, and still insists on joining us on all these walks.

The Wicked Wet Wood (Walk 6) has lulled many a person into a sense of security during some recent dry spells. It has taken its revenge by all but swallowing them up next time they attempt it after the rains.

David Dickenson, *Spring 1991*

CONTENTS

Page

HOW TO USE THIS BOOK   6

FINDING YOUR WAY   7

MAP   *8-9*

WALKS 1-28   *11-51*

WALKS 1A-28A   *54-90*

HOW TO USE THIS BOOK

In my ramblings through the Forest, I rarely set out with the intention of going from point A to point B, but select a variety of criss-cross paths as the mood takes me that day. This is the natural way to enjoy the beauty of the Forest and this book is designed to help you take your walks in a similar ad-hoc fashion, with the certainty (well, likelihood!) of ending back at your starting point.

There are 5 starting points (accessible by road) for the walks in this book:

Lyndhurst — **(WALKS 1** and **2).**

Ashurst — **(WALK 25A**, starting from the garden stile of the New Forest Hotel).

Matley Wood Camp Site — **(WALKS 16, 27, 22A** and **28A,** all starting at the track 80 paces from the campsite entrance along the road towards Lyndhurst).

Denny Lodge Camp Site — **(WALKS 22, 20A** and **21A,** all starting from where the campsite track joins the main road).

Beaulieu Road — **(WALKS 20, 21** and **19A,** all starting from Shatterford Bottom carpark).

Each WALK is just one part of your day's excursion, which can be as long or as short as you like. Choose your starting point, and then design the journey as you go along. At the end of each WALK you will be given a series of Options to choose from, each one showing the *minimum* time it will take you from that point to reach Lyndhurst or Ashurst. As you progress, you can increase or decrease your distance from base according to your mood (and feet!).

Each WALK has a number, so that you can follow it on the map (page 8-9). The walk in the opposite direction to the arrow on the map bears the same number followed by the letter **"A"**. The **"A" WALKS** are to be found in the second half of the book. The text in lighter print is mainly descriptive, and not vital for route-finding.

FOOTWEAR

The New Forest is often wet underfoot, so wellingtons will ensure a more relaxing walk in all but the driest of times. However, a comfortable pair of strong shoes will suffice for most of the year.

FINDING YOUR WAY

The direction you should take at the start of each **WALK** is described in the text and confirmed by a SILVA Compass Reference number (ie. the magnetic bearing in degrees). SILVA compasses are highly recommended to all walkers and are widely available at camping/outdoor shops.

METHOD

1. Turn the dial until the required number (see "Compass Ref." at the heading of each **WALK**) is aligned with the index line on the compass.

2. Without changing the dial setting, turn the entire compass horizontally until the red end of the magnetic needle aligns with the arrow in the dial housing beneath it.

3. Walk in the direction indicated by the travel arrow.

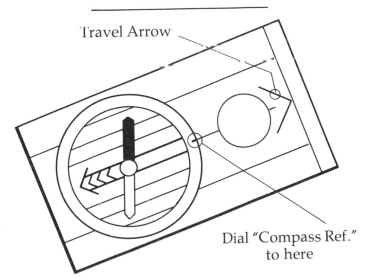

Travel Arrow

Dial "Compass Ref." to here

A SILVA Compass

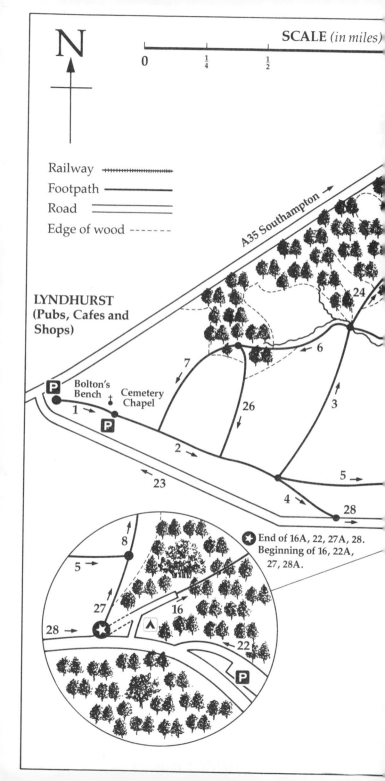

SCALE *(in miles)*

0   ¼   ½

Railway
Footpath
Road
Edge of wood

LYNDHURST
(Pubs, Cafes and
Shops)

A35 Southampton

24

7

6

P   Bolton's
         Bench   Cemetery
1   Chapel
    P
                         26
              2

              23   3

                                    5
                                4
                                        28

8

5   ⭐ End of 16A, 22, 27A, 28.
                                    Beginning of 16, 22A,
                                    27, 28A.

27   16

28 →   22

                                        P

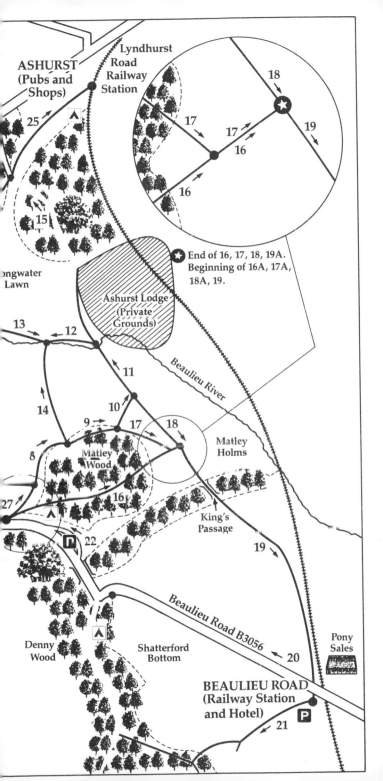

ASHURST
(Pubs and
Shops)

25

15

Lyndhurst
Road
Railway
Station

18

17

17

16

19

16

End of 16, 17, 18, 19A.
Beginning of 16A, 17A,
18A, 19.

ongwater
Lawn

Ashurst Lodge
(Private
Grounds)

13

12

11

Beaulieu River

14

10

9

17

18

Matley
Wood

Matley
Holms

8

27

16

King's
Passage

22

19

Beaulieu Road B3056

Denny
Wood

Shatterford
Bottom

20

Pony
Sales

BEAULIEU ROAD
(Railway Station
and Hotel)

P

21

The enchanting Woodland...

Discover the secret world of Britain's best loved forest with this infinitely detailed Outdoor Leisure Map from Ordnance Survey.

Features include a wealth of tourist information including camping and caravan sites, picnic areas, viewpoints, footpaths and those important rights of way.

Available from bookshops and stationers throughout Britain.

Ordnance Survey
OUTDOOR LEISURE 22
New Forest
Includes Southampton, Ringwood, Lymington, C...
and part of Bournemouth

A specially designe...
popular recreational a...

2½ in to 1 mile

1:25 000

New Forest Ponies
Hampshire

Walk 1

Park at Boltons Bench car park. Turn your back on Lyndhurst village and stroll up the tarmac track.

This short stretch has always attracted large numbers of visitors and is usually bustling with ponies and people. Its popularity goes back through Victorian times (when hordes of picknickers roamed the area with their butterfly nets) to 1688, when Lord Bolton was considerate enough to provide the first bench round the ring of ancient yew trees on the burial mound to your right. In winter, the steep slope of this mound provides local enthusiasts with one of the best tobogganing runs in the entire Forest.

In summer, however, your attention will more naturally be drawn towards the green ahead, where can be found the true essence of rural England: a splendidly thatched cricket pavilion commanding a well-loved pitch. When a match is in progress, the undulating contours of the field and the occasional pony cropping the turf at backward square leg add much to the rustic charm.

Continuing up the slope takes you towards an old stone wall against which children play a less formal brand of cricket. The wall encloses a delightful little chapel and a cemetery, seen to best advantage in springtime, when the daffodils are blooming.

You have now reached the upper car park, which is the start of WALK 2.

Options

a) **OK — you've had enough — turn around and go back again.** (*5 mins from base*).
b) **Continue with WALK 2** (*35 mins to Lyndhurst, 60 mins to Ashurst*).

Walk 2

If you decided to miss out WALK 1 you will have arrived here by car, having driven up from Boltons Bench along the tarmac sloping gently up towards the cemetery and cricket pavilion.

Take the broad gravel track that leads straight on from the tarmac path up onto the Ridgeway. The views are extensive in all directions, with vast open tracts of heather, unrivalled anywhere for colour in late summer.

Let the kids play hide-and-seek amongst the gorse bushes with their scented yellow flowers — there are several closely parallel tracks, all up on the ridge, so it is difficult for them to get lost. Just out of sight on your right are several huge sand-pits where they will play contentedly for hours if you give them the chance.

The concrete block visible on your right shortly after the start is a Trig. point, used as a reference point by the Ordinance Survey to ensure accuracy in their maps. It's hard to say why people enjoy climbing on it, since the view is much the same. Perhaps it's just the exhilaration which comes from treading on Government property.

After a while you will find yourself walking in a series of ruts, unless you have followed the kink to the right in the main path, which takes

on the left. Two other smaller tracks also join us at this spot, and it's time to choose your next option.

you a few feet above them. Either route will do, since they soon rejoin, leading steeply downhill and then levelling out again. You are approaching the point where another broad track leads off downhill from the Ridgeway

Options

a) Retrace your steps — WALK 2A *(15 mins to Lyndhurst, 45 mins to Ashurst).*
b) Continue on the broad track as it bears slightly right — WALK 4 *(35 mins to Lyndhurst, 60 mins to Ashurst).*
c) Want to see the promised land? Turn left for WALK 3 *(60 mins to Lyndhurst, 45 mins to Ashurst).*
d) Fancy a lonely pony track across the moor, leading to an interesting wood? WALK 5 *(45 mins to Lyndhurst, 70 mins to Ashurst).*

Walk 3

Downhill all the way, with a distant view of a peaceful river meandering through a verdant strip in the valley bottom. Straight ahead can be seen one of the most attractive clumps of firs in the Forest.

This long straight path is part of the old SALT WAY, running from the ancient salt works at Lymington to Southampton (these works were already in decline 200 years ago).

About 100 paces after beginning the descent, a long thin strip of coppice with its roots deep in water begins on the left and runs parallel to the path for some way. It comprises a curious collection of scrubby trees that thrive in the wet — fascinat-

ing to a naturalist, but potentially fatal to inspect at close quarters.

Now is the time to point out the important distinction between MUD and BOG. Please pay careful attention as your life may depend on it! MUD is merely wet dirt: on this path you will soon become well acquainted with it. It contains little organic matter but has an honest character and is easy enough to spot. Mud asks for, and indeed, should be given no respect.

BOG, however, demands your greatest respect. It is usually disguised by sundry plants, and is composed primarily of decaying vegetation. Being thus highly deficient in nitrogen, it tries to

remedy this by sucking down all forms of animal life — including YOU! In winter, long strips of bog can often be recognised from a distance by their colourful red and yellow tints. In the summer, the bright green Sphagnum moss can be seen at the base of the heather. If this moss is squeezed, masses of water will pour down into your boots. This fluid absorbency made it much used during the First World War as a dressing in place of cotton wool. Also found here and there in Forest bogs are the little red rosettes of the Sundew plant. Rare elsewhere in Britain, the Sundew is noted for its sticky hairs which trap and eat insects. The shrub Bog Myrtle is often present too, and the odd lonely Pine may also be seen struggling for life. The pretty yellow stars of the sedge, together with club mosses and purple-flowered Marsh Gentian, add even further interest. Cotton-Grass, with its distinctive white tufts, appears in the worst areas. All bogs should be avoided, but never venture into one where Cotton-Grass is growing.

Once past the stand of fir-trees on the left, the mud across the path increases, although it usually remains negotiable. The bog on the left deepens and another one appears on your right. The

Myrtle bushes are more vigorous here, about 3 foot in height, and with a delicious fragrance – crush a few leaves in the palm of your hand. They start with beautiful fresh green buds in spring, turning darker throughout the summer and autumn before being shed. Another colour to note here is the rich brown of the streams, due to the high levels of tannin present in peat.

You now reach a delightful stream with a bridge over the young Beaulieu river. Relax a while – laze out and read the introduction to WALK 13 before choosing one of the options below.

Options

a) How about following this stream, perhaps to see the deer at sunset, or the mists at sunrise? WALK 13 *(60 mins to Lyndhurst, 40 mins to Ashurst).*
b) Prefer the shelter of a wood with a pub in prospect? WALK 24 *(95 mins to Lyndhurst, 30 mins to Ashurst).*
c) A little on the wild side!! WALK 6 (if you dare!) *(35 mins to Lyndhurst, 70 mins to Ashurst).*

"Mud asks for, and should be given, no respect."

Walk 4

8 minutes

Compass Ref:130

This broad track continues gently uphill along the ridgeway, with the steeple of Lyndhurst Church (where Alice Hargreaves, the inspiration for Alice-in-Wonderland, is buried) behind you. After a short while, you reach the Lyndhurst/Beaulieu road. If you have dogs with you, put them on the lead at this point.

This stretch is particularly pleasant for those of a gregarious nature, because lots of people walk along it throughout the year. Even so, no amount of company can spoil the very fine panorama on your left as you approach the road.

When you reach the road you will see a group of three silver birch trees springing out of the ground in close companionship. Choose your next option.

Options

a) **Either retrace your steps — WALKS 4A then 2A or go back along the road — WALK 23.** *Both are only 30 mins to Lyndhurst, but 95 mins to Ashurst.*
b) **Turn left onto WALK 28** *(45 mins to Lyndhurst, 60 mins to Ashurst).*

Walk 5

A lovely walk, this, along a narrow track made for ponies, not people. Young lovers can hold hands only with difficulty.

Start off across the heath along the narrow track pointing off diagonally between the broad ridgeway path and

tive cry will draw your attention to them as they circle round high in the sky, way above the darting lapwings. Borrow your partner's binoculars for a close-up of their long distinctive downward curving beaks.

Start of Walk 5

the equally broad downhill track on the left. The neat roundness of Matley Wood is dead ahead in the distance. Keep straight, ignoring any tracks which branch off in other directions.

This area of heath is much used by deer, which cross your path to reach the river in the valley low down on your left. It's unusual to spot them when the sun is high, but if your dog darts off suddenly, he may well have picked up their scent. Curlews nest in the moist bogland in the bottom on the left (in this part of the world a "bottom" is a boggy valley). Their distinc-

The track eventually comes out onto the broad grassy ring-road that circles Matley Wood, which is 200 paces dead ahead. Take your next option.

Options

a) Turn right to the road and Matley Wood campsite — WALK 27A *(35 mins to Lyndhurst, 55 mins to Ashurst).*
b) Turn left along the woodland edge — WALK 8 *(60 mins to Lyndhurst, 50 mins to Ashurst).*

The Cemetery Firs

Walk 6

Compass Ref:285

This subtle route takes us through the Wicked Wet Wood, and is designed for the young at heart. You will need a pair of wellies and a good sense of humour.

Starting from the bridge over the stream, with the water running from right to left, cross the bridge and turn right. Continue upstream, ignoring the next bridge.

It is a matter of fine judgement which side of the bank is the least treacherous at any one time. No two months are ever the same, although the left bank tends to be easier than the right bank for most of the journey. Sometimes
the driest part is the middle of the stream. Do not dive into the bog-myrtle (the surrounding scrub bushes) — what appears to be easy at first soon becomes dangerous bog, and you cannot retrace your steps.

Those who survive this difficult approach will now reach the Wicked Wet Wood. This is the most miserable, wretched, evil-smelling, evil-natured wood you are likely to meet, so treasure the moment well.

It is perpetually damp: light trying to filter through its twisted stunted branches is snatched at and never reaches down to its lower

members. This is just as well, for its lower members can only be dimly perceived prising themselves out of a flatulent greasy bogland so foul that the only greenery present is the mould and slime covering unfamiliar excrescences. Even the tree roots can be seen attempting to escape upwards out of the slime and filth. Wildlife enters the wood to die, and then only if desperate. Long spindly branches snatch at your hair constantly, even though you are forced to a constant stoop. Should you get lost just follow the line of hairnets snatched from my mother-in-law's head over the passage of time.

The stream should be followed up through the wood by walking along its bed. The left bank can be attempted, but only after a prolonged drought or a prolonged freeze. The stream bed is firm gravel, and reasonably easy to negotiate if you stick to the shallows. There are occasional spots of deep sinking clay however, including one at a crucial point where it is desirable to use the overhead branches for support.

This Dante-esque experience is over quite quickly, and you reach a large rectangle of open green sward surrounded on three sides by the Wicked Wet Wood.

Exit from the wood

Cross this rectangle diagonally to the hummock at the opposite point, where you will come across a broad path.

Options

a) An easy, attractive path — WALK 7 *(20 mins to Lyndhurst, 80 mins to Ashurst)*.
b) Take the pony track across the heath — WALK 26 *(30 mins to Lyndhurst, 75 mins to Ashurst)*.

Walk 7

A pleasant uphill track, broad and easy all the way. With the tall holly hedges on two sides of the green rectangle behind you, follow the track up through the pine wood. It soon opens out onto a heathland slope. On the left is a small deep pond, which is rapidly becoming shallower as it fills up with sticks that my dog has failed to retrieve after insisting I throw them in for her to fetch.

As you puff and pant your way uphill, notice the firs in the middle distance on your right, reaching up from the tombstones of the cemetery close to the Lyndhurst base. They display a superb range of evergreen tones and forms, and provide a useful landmark for those who wander off route.

This path is attractive right up to the ridgeway, but those wishing to avoid the crowds can strike off towards the left-hand side of the cemetery firs — there are many easy sandy tracks between the heather, but the gorse bushes occasionally get too big for their boots and attack you.

On reaching the broad ridgeway track, you are in the middle of WALK 2.

Options

a) **Turn right** — *(10 mins to Lyndhurst, 65 mins to Ashurst).*
b) **Turn left to complete WALK 2 should you wish to delve further into the Lyndhurst triangle** *(55 mins to Ashurst).*

"The pond is rapidly filling up with sticks which my dog
has failed to retrieve."

Walk 8

Follow the broad green track gently downhill, with the gorse windbreak on the left and Matley Wood about 200 paces on your right.

The approach to the wood shows off the wide variety of our smaller native trees which can be found at a woodland edge. Blossom trees such as crab-apple, hawthorn and blackthorn mingle with the grace of the silver birch, above a carpet of fern and heather.

As the track curves more sharply to the right, the wood on your right gets closer. Just as you merge into the edge of the wood itself, another path crosses from out of the wood and runs down the heath on the left. Stop here.

Options

a) **Turn left for WALK 14** *(50 mins to Lyndhurst, 45 mins to Ashurst).*
b) **Continue straight on with WALK 9** *(60 mins to Lyndhurst, 45 mins to Ashurst).*

Walk 9

Start of Walk 9

A naturalist's delight. Follow the broad, often muddy track round the lower edge of Matley Wood. The thin strip of wood on the left abounds in a wide variety of mushrooms and toadstools amongst the ferns. The woodland edge is abruptly cut off by sloping boggy heathland.

Many people, myself included, are fascinated by the bracket fungi sometimes found on Silver Birches in this area. The birch is perhaps the most graceful of the Forest trees, with its delicate, drooping, burgundy-coloured branches contrasting all year round with the silvery white bark. On the face of it, the bracket fungi add a touch of fairyland charm to the scene. Each one takes the form of an enormous whitish mushroom which has been chopped in half and stuck firmly onto the side of the tree. That creamy blob is actually the fruiting body of a fungus whose evil filaments have already spread deep inside the trunk, condemning the tree to an early demise. It is the main killer of Silver Birches, and explains why old ones are rarely seen — especially on a woodland edge, where they are more prone to the sort of damage which allows fungal spores to enter.

However, self-sown Silver Birches are superb colonisers of grassland, as you see here; the many new saplings combine with bracken and bramble to give protective cover for some of our grander trees, which years later take full advantage of the newly opened skies when the Silver Birch comes tumbling down. Following a line from your left to your right will give you an excellent illustration of this gradual grassland-to-forest transformation.

The path forks as it approaches the corner of the wood; take the right fork. After 60 paces you will come to a cross-path as a path comes down out of the woods. Choose your next Option here.

Options

a) **A visit to the attractive Beaulieu river — WALK 10** (*55 mins to Lyndhurst, 40 mins to Ashurst*).
b) **Return to Lyndhurst through Matley Wood or an extended walk to the pub at Beaulieu Road — WALK 17** (*35 mins to Lyndhurst, 45 mins to Beaulieu Road*).

Walk 10

This track leads increasingly downhill, with heath on the right and a good example of bog-land on the left.

W.H. Rogers, in his Victorian ' Guide to the New Forest' was also concerned about the dangers of bogs, and records "in the hunting season it is not uncommon to hear of another sportsman becoming unpleasantly acquainted with them, as their surface may be mistaken for a piece of green turf offering a short cut. In these cases, it requires the use of strong ropes and the aid of several men to extricate the horseman from the deep black slush into which he may have sunk to the saddle".

On your left you will see a mound — one of many to be found in the New Forest. They are Stone Age barrows, and were filled with urns containing the cremated remains of our ancestors. They were referred to as barrows until John R. Wise excavated many of them in the 1840's *(see his book 'The New Forest, Its History and Scenery')* since when the Ordnance Survey has labelled them 'tumuli' in recognition of their changed state.

Just after the mound, your path merges with a similar path coming down from the right. This forms the next option point.

Options

a) Continue downhill — WALK 11 *(60 mins to Lyndhurst, 35 mins to Ashurst).*

b) Take the other fork (uphill) — WALK 18 *(50 mins to Lyndhurst, 55 mins to Ashurst).*

Walk 11

Continue downhill to the bridge over the river. Close to the river, on your right, is a large mound tantalisingly labelled "earthworks" on the Ordnance Survey map. This is a grand place to loll in the ferns in summer providing you are fond of flies.

If you remain awake, you will notice two kinds of flies. The first, similar to the common house fly, is a great tease — as Hudson wrote in HAMPSHIRE DAYS, "they simply buzz around without an object — flies that have no beauty, no lancet to stab you with and no distinction of any kind, yet will persist in forcing themselves on your attention". (Hudson had a pretty similar view of Hampshire folk too.) The other species you are likely to meet is the biting horse fly, which is much easier to swat. Two of Hudson's favourite pastimes were to sit for hours beside graves, especially the Forest's ancient barrows, and "swat those horse-flies inflicting the sharpest bites upon my legs, and throw them into the stream for the minnows to eat". On this mound you can admirably combine both pastimes.

Having tired of these pursuits, drop down to the bridge and select an option.

Options

**a) Return to Lyndhurst —
WALK 12** (*55 mins to Lyndhurst, 55 mins to Ashurst*).
b) Skirt the edge of Ashurst Lodge — WALK 15 (*55 mins to Lyndhurst, 30 mins to Ashurst*).

Walk 12

Cross the bridge (the water flowing under you from left to right) and turn left to follow the Beaulieu river upstream to the next bridge. A less interesting but drier alternative is to follow the opposite bank which is your right, its man-made straightness contrasting with the meanderings of the natural river, you are faced with two choices - (i) one tremendous leap, (ii) follow the ditch up to one of two small bridges.

Bridge over the Beaulieu River (end of Walk 12)

the official path, and includes a small bridge over a tributary.

You are now on the Longwater Lawn, which extends to the Colbury boundary stone (end of WALK 13A). This is one of my favourite spots in the Forest.

Keep a short distance from the river, and pick your footsteps carefully in the winter. There is no regular path to follow. When you reach the ditch entering the river from

Either way, cross to the other side of the ditch and continue to the next bridge across the river. Here you can choose your next option.

Options

a) Carry straight on for the most gentle riverside stroll of your life — WALK 13A *(45 mins to Lyndhurst, 40 mins to Ashurst).*
b) Head for Matley Wood — WALK 14A *(45 mins to Lyndhurst, 75 mins to Ashurst).*

The Beaulieu River (Walk 12)

Walk 13

Cross the bridge (the river flowing under you from left to right) and turn right to follow the river bank.

This is an excellent place to dawdle, if you are so inclined. Take off your socks and shoes and dangle your toes among the minnows while water boatmen and water beetles scurry across the surface. The kids can safely paddle in the gravel-bedded stream and gather wild watercress for your salad. Beside the bank can be seen two boundary stones, useful landmarks for the old-time salt traders as they crossed the bridge from Lyndhurst to Colbury Parish. Upstream of the bridge, where the waters are deeper, a carpet of white stars is formed by the flowers of the Water Crowsfoot.

Set off along the left bank of the river. This broad strip of green, called Longwater

Boundary stones (start of Walk 13)

Lawn, is kept free from heather and shrubs by grazing ponies and cattle. Several times at sunset, we have seen a dozen or more stags strolling down from the heath on the right, pausing to drink before moving on across the flat plain to the woods on the distant left. They may be either spotted Fallow deer, distinguishable by the broad antlers of the male, or Red deer, with round, pointed branching antlers. The males of both species shed their antlers after the late summer rutting season, whereupon the females desert them and graze in unisex groups. The shy white-rumped Roe deer, or the even smaller and more elusive Muntjac deer may also be seen occasionally. The rare Sika deer is not to be found here, preferring the flatter, low-lying areas north-east of Brockenhurst. However the observant traveller will rarely not be rewarded with some glimpse of deer on a day's walk anywhere in the Forest, even with a boisterous dog or two as company.

Keep a lookout for a large solitary rounded sloe bush on this bank — it has a hollowed-out centre for its animal inhabitants, but is rich in sloe berries in autumn, following a brilliant white show of spring blackthorn blossom. It's a good place to collect berries for your sloe gin, provided the squirrels don't get there first.

Shortly after the river is obscured by trees, you come to a bridge over the river and you must now make a further choice.

Options

a) A visit to Matley Wood — WALK 14A *(50 mins to Lyndhurst, 50 mins to Ashurst).*
b) Continue along the stream — WALK 12A *(60 mins to Lyndhurst, 40 mins to Ashurst).*

Walk 14

Turn your back on Matley Wood and take the broad track that passes through a gap in the trees and downhill over the heath.

This walk is easy and straight all the way, and a very good place to learn about the different types of heather to be found in the Forest. Studying heather is somewhat boring if it's not in flower, so skip this section if you can't see purple spots before your eyes. There are three main types: Ling, Cross-leaved heath and Bell-heather. LING (Calluna vulgaris) is the most common, having small mid-purple flowers on the upper half of its outer stem. It is fairly tolerant of wet or dry conditions, and is thus to be found giving the main colour to both the high and low ground. The more retiring CROSS-LEAVED HEATH (Erica tetralix) has clusters of larger, soft pink, bell-shaped flowers at the top of its stems and is to be found in smaller groups in the wetter areas (such as the lower slopes here). The third variety, BELL HEATHER (Erica cinerea), is my favourite. It prefers the dry, higher areas and gives a wonderful splash of colour to the ridgeway at Lyndhurst, before yielding to the softer coloured Ling in autumn. If your companion is being smug and claims to already know the different heathers, challenge him/her to identify them by smell alone.

Providing you have not been stung by a bee while sniffing the heather, you now reach the bridge that passes over the stream. Cross over and you are already into your next option.

Options

a) Turn left and follow a lazy Forest stream — WALK 13A *(45 mins to Lyndhurst, 40 mins to Ashurst).*
b) Turn right — WALK 12A *(60 mins to Lyndhurst, 40 mins to Ashurst).*

"See if your companion can identify the heathers by smell alone."

Walk 15

Standing on the bridge with the water flowing from left to right under you, you will see a wide path ahead. Take it.

After a time, the path curves to the right as it goes uphill towards the railings which enclose the grounds of Ashurst Lodge. The rhododendrons of the lodge have spilled over the railings and the wild escapees provide a beautiful display of flowers in May — their shapes contrasting with the heavy formality of those behind bars. As you follow the railings round, note the ancient hollies. Their age reflects the old custom of waiting until a holly tree showed signs of decay and then chopping it back hard one winter. This operation provided valuable browsing for the deer and also rejuvenated the tree, and was repeated roughly every 30 years. The custom ceased as interest in deer-keeping declined, so that old holly trees were sadly neglected until the Victorians took up the noble art of berry-worshipping at Christmas.

Follow the path to the right as it curves round the grounds and you will see a leafy glade by the gates of Ashurst Lodge. Turn left through the woods along the tarmac drive, bearing in mind some cars do actually use this road. The woods on either side are excellent for blackberrying in autumn and observing weird and wonderful fungi. When the trees disappear on the left, you will notice an iron trough in the open heather, used as a watering hole by the ponies.

The water trough (Walk 15)

The trees then desert you on the right also; shortly before a ramp across the road you will reach a low Forestry access gate guarding a track on the left. Stop! Your options here will be dictated by the time of day.

Options

a) Pub lunch? turn right — WALK 25 *(75 mins to Lyndhurst, 10 mins to Ashurst).*
b) Return to Lyndhurst on WALK 24A *(55 mins to Lyndhurst, 70 mins to Ashurst).*

Walk 16

Facing away from Lyndhurst take the wide track leading off the road to the left towards Matley Wood and the campsite. This is only a small campsite, but if you tarry and change direction, you may miss the correct path out.

Close to the waste disposal area is a low Forestry access gate across the path which enters the wood. Follow this path.

This is a fascinating wood, although only a teenager compared to other woods in the area. There is evidence from an old bank that it was enclosed in medieval times, probably as an encoppicement to form a mixture of low-growing trees (for browsing and fuel) and a few full grown trees to meet the limited demand for timber. However, it has not been legally enclosed to grow timber since Parliament first voted on such matters in 1669. The remains of this medieval copse, in the form of some giant pollarded beeches, can be seen through the trees on your left as you go downhill. But the main character of the wood is given by the oaks and (unusual for the Forest) sweet chestnut. The largest of these were planted about 200 years ago, but many generations of self-sown youngsters can also be seen.

Opportunist hollies complete the picture. Children (and myself) take great delight in testing their skills by stripping the green from a chestnut leaf to leave a 'herring bone' of veins — there are usually about 30 veins to the leaf-stalk, with the first 29 remaining nicely in place, but the 30th insisting on coming away with the green. You then have to select another innocent leaf to prove you can really do it. Chestnut compares poorly for wood production; although as durable as oak, it tends to crack during seasoning — useful plank lengths are thus so short that its main use was for coffin making!

Towards the bottom of the wood, an ancient yew can be seen a few paces in on the left, quite out of place. What rituals were played out on this spot? Prior to the building up of the wood during medieval times, the mists rolling up the slopes from the boggy valley bottom must have created quite an atmosphere. Until recently 2 tall exotic oaks stood by this path. Their huge leaves on long stalks identifying them as Red Oaks from North America, perhaps planted by a gentleman on his return from the New World. The grander of the 2 fell in a hurricane in October 1988 having just reached its centenary.

As you leave the wood and pass out onto the heath, ignore a track on the right. A little further on, a broad track crosses your path — ignore this too, and the next, less well defined path as it crosses yours some 40 paces further on. Finally, 80 paces past this is a good cross-roads, with a fine track to the left leading clearly over the heath to the left of a wood in the mid distance. Ensure you are at this cross-roads before determining your next option.

Options

a) Turn left across the heath to the river — WALK 18A *(65 mins to Lyndhurst, 40 mins to Ashurst)*.
b) Tempted to visit the attractive fringe of Matley Wood? Double back on WALK 17A *(50 mins to Lyndhurst, 45 mins to Ashurst)*.
c) Want to examine the King's Passage? Take WALK 19 which will also reward you with some fine grassland plains *(90 mins to Lyndhurst, 90 mins to Ashurst)*.

Entrance to Matley Wood (Walk 16)

Walk 17

As you face up the path leading into the centre of Matley Wood, take the path on the left (you may be at one of two points 40 paces apart which appear as cross-roads or T-junctions according to the time of the year, but both tracks off left soon meet as you skirt the edge of the wood).

The trees quickly thin out; the path runs through a short strip of gorse between two handsome Scots pines.

These Scots pines are fine examples of the lucky escapees from the formal pine enclosures, which have celebrated by taking on such a grand variety of shapes that they are scarcely recognizable as the same species. But note the distinctive reddish bark, often shedding in patches, and contrasting with their rich, green leaves. Their tendency to be solitary and have such individually characteristic shapes makes them useful as landmarks throughout the Forest, especially in winter. Following some scatter-brained navigation, I have often been relieved to catch sight of one of my old Scots friends in the distance. If you know their exact whereabouts on the Ordnance Survey map (it is worth marking a few), a compass bearing will soon show you your whereabouts.

Pass through the short strip of gorse onto the heathland, with some not-so-attractive views of pylons in the distance. There are a lot of paths around here, so take care with the navigating. 170 paces past the gorse, on the heathland, a broad path crosses yours. Turn left onto this. Count 120 paces (ignoring a cross-track at an angle) and another path crosses yours at right angles. Stop here. A track on your left can be seen running down over the heath to the left of a wood in the mid-distance.

Options

a) Want to visit the heart of Matley Wood? Double back on WALK 16A *(45 mins to Lyndhurst, 70 mins to Ashurst).*

b) Take the left turn down the heath to the river — WALK 18A *(65 mins to Lyndhurst, 40 mins to Ashurst.*

c) Want to examine the King's Passage? Turn right for WALK 19, which will also reward you with some fine grassland plains *(90 mins to Lyndhurst, 90 mins to Ashurst).*

Walk 18

Take the left-hand fork as it leads uphill.

As you walk up this delightful heather-clad slope, take a close look at those pretty pink flowers. If you see a bee which is not as busy as bees are supposed to be, the odds are that he has just become the next meal of a Crab Spider. A few silken threads may already be woven across his body, and close inspection will reveal a set of jaws and eight skinny legs encompassing him as well. What you are unlikely to notice, no more than the unfortunate bee did, is that one of those pink-shaped flowers is actually the body of the spider! This Moriarty of the Forest is an expert at camouflage, blending equally with tree bark or the bright colours of an alluring flower, depending on his chosen site. He can also change the size and shape of his belly, an attribute likely to be envied by the female of our species!

The track, previously so decent, becomes swallowed up in mud towards the top, but it doesn't last long. You will soon reach a main track crossing yours just before a few gorse bushes. These mark the boundary between the heath and a grassy plain. Stop at this cross-roads.

Options

a) Want to examine the King's Passage? Take WALK 19, which will also reward you with some fine grassland plains *(90 mins to Lyndhurst, 90 mins to Ashurst).*
b) Tempted by the fringe of Matley Wood? Turn right onto WALK 17A *(55 mins to Lyndhurst, 45 mins to Ashurst).*

Walk 19

30 minutes

Compass Ref:140

A beautiful open stretch of easy walking this, well worth the time spent. Take the level path that pops out through a line of gorse onto a large flat area of grass.

This attractive plain is Matley Holms. A 'holm' or 'lawn' is the local name for such a feature, and this is the first of two you will cross on this walk. The grass is kept free of heathers and gorse by the close grazing of cattle, ponies and deer. There is a very delicate ecological balance at work here, and any change in the numbers of grazing animals (ponies giving a more effective short back and sides) would soon upset it. Note the many colourful plants among the different grasses, and also that moles enjoy destroying these lawns every bit as much as they do yours at home!

The King's Passage (Walk 19)

A thin strip of wood protecting a river forms the opposite border of this plain, and you must take an imaginary path leading to a gap in the trees half-way along. As you get close to the trees, you will spot the gap, with an obvious path running through it. There is no danger of mistaking the way — elsewhere the inpenetrable wooded strip encloses an equally unfordable stream.

You have now reached the King's Passage. Those wishing to dawdle before tackling the mud can treat themselves to a game of Pooh Sticks on the first bridge. Everything necessary is to hand — deep flowing water, a rail to lean over and a plentiful supply of sticks.

Having successfully negotiated the second bridge, the path leads out onto another lawn. Almost immediately on your left is a very small, harmless-looking pond; don't be tempted onto it if frozen over. It is very deep

and desperately cold when the ice breaks (note — not if, but when!).

On the opposite side of this grassy plain can be seen a heather-clad bank forming the distant border, and on your left, the South-ampton to Bournemouth railway forming another bor-der. Take a diagonal route to where these two meet, and you will find a good sandy path leading moderately uphill.

The ponies you will see on the lawn live wild, but are owned by Commoners — local residents who still exer-cise their ancient right to graze their animals on the Forest pastures. (This right is attached to the hearth, not the family). Each area of the Forest has its own fashion in pony tails — they are clipped in autumn into distinctive layers, gradually growing out into functioning fly-swats the following summer. The foals are sold off at pony sales which are held several times a year at a site which you can visit at the end of this walk.

Continue up the track, with the railway line on your left until you come to the road.

Options

a) Turn left over the bridge for a pint at the excellent Beaulieu Hotel (open all day). Return to this point to recommence walking.

b) Take the easy road back — WALK 20 *(60 mins to Lyndhurst, 85 mins to Ashurst).*

c) An interesting return via Denny Wood — WALK 22 *(70 mins to Lyndhurst, 95 mins to Ashurst).*

"Note that moles enjoy destroying these lawns as much
as they do yours at home."

Walk 20

This is a road route for those short of time or energy; it passes through attractive scenery, but you have to put up with the traffic. From Shatterford car park, turn left along the tarmac road to Lyndhurst and stay on the right-hand side grass verge all the way.

Much of the scenery on the right is hidden by a small raised area, but there are extensive views over the bogland (called Shatterford Bottom) to the left.

You may remember as a teenager playing the game of 'points', whereby you score so many points for running over a cat, a few more for a dog, and so on up the scale. On this stretch of road, I regret to say, the game is played for real. Being straight, narrow and unfenced, it's an easy place to pile up the points; and judging from the statistics of slaughtered ponies hereabouts, some people have achieved high scores.

The road eventually curves to the left, and at the next sharp bend to the right, a small tarmac track on the left leads off to Denny Wood campsite. Choose your next option.

Options

a) Follow the main road for a short stretch — WALK 22 *(40 mins to Lyndhurst, 65 mins to Ashurst).*
b) Turn left to explore Denny Wood — WALK 21A *(120 mins to Lyndhurst, 100 mins to Ashurst).*

Walk 21

A highly attractive route, with a mixture of heath and ancient oak/beech woodland.

At Shatterford car park, two paths run off from the pines and picnic tables. Ignore the left-hand one, running close to the railway line; take the path on the right that strikes off across a flattish heath towards Denny Wood in the distance.

The track crosses Shatterford Bottom by a wooden bridge. This bridge is especially welcome, because the Bottom forms a ring with Matley Bog and Stephill Bottom, creating one of the most impenetrable areas in the Forest. Look for the white tufts of Cotton Grass — a true danger signal. Keep your dogs out; if they don't get swallowed up in the mire, you will almost wish they had been — they will come up smelling not of roses but of rotten eggs.

Away to your left can be seen the edge of Bishop's Dyke — a raised heather-clad wall and ditch surrounding a swampy area which until recently was owned by the Bishop of Winchester. On inspection, you may feel that he is welcome to it. It was originally granted by Edward I in 1284 — legend has it that the Bishop was offered as much land as he could crawl around on hands and knees in one day. Its erratic shape and swampy nature suggest that he may have been a keen wild-fowler and/or a drunkard.

The path forks shortly before it reaches the wood. Take the right-hand fork, and on entering the wood proper you will find your now narrowed track crossed by another one, equally narrow. Turn right here and continue into the wood. At this point, the path rapidly declines to a state where it barely exists. But all you have to do is keep the edge of the wood in view on your right, with the heath and bogland beyond it. The wood is very open and easy to stroll through and you will soon reach a tarmac path which crosses yours roughly at a right-angle. Under no circumstances try to cross the boggy heath on the right.

The wood is a lovely mixture of trees of various ages, most about two hundred years old but some much more than that. It used to be called the Cathedral Beeches because of the graceful arches of beech lining your way. The drought of 1976, and the storms of 1988 and 1990 have severely depleted the wood. While many of the fallen are eventually sawn up and carted off, the less obstructive are left to rot down and give birth to further life again in a few years time.

One of the old tree stumps along here had a sign on it saying "Death And Decay", which gave my wife and me a good laugh when we first saw it. That was fifteen years ago, and ever since the laugh has been on us — we cannot pass a crumbling tree-stump nowadays without mentally labelling it 'death and decay'. This is just what the original author intended; he revealed a fascinating new world to us, a twilight underworld of beasts and bugs all co-operating in the work of destruction, and multiplying in their turn to become food for other life in the Forest. Every fallen tree or stump has a different but enchanting colony of its own, one in which mosses and lichens join with woodlice and beetles and ferns and fungi.

When you reach the tarmac path, turn right and follow it through Denny Lodge campsite to the road. Because of the surrounding bogland, the next two options both involve some road-walking.

Options

a) **Turn left for a short stretch of road before Matley Wood — WALK 22** *(40 mins to Lyndhurst, 65 mins to Ashurst).*
b) **Turn right towards Beaulieu Road station — WALK 20A** *(90 mins to Lyndhurst, 85 mins to Ashurst).*

Walk 22

With the tarmac track to Denny Wood campsite on your left, start walking up the road. Very shortly, on the right-hand side of the road can be seen the remains of the old road, with a little bridge over a tributary. Leave the tarmac road to follow this.

This is a good point at which to admire the stream, which is a tributary of the Beaulieu river. Relax on the grass and peel an orange, but resist the temptation to paddle; the river-bed has some unexpected deep pockets, which shift from season to season. What is safe for the children one month may be the end of them the next.

Follow the old road, which leads into a car-park and then becomes tarmac again. This leads you up to the main road once more — continue in this direction (the old road can still be made out if you keep on the right-hand grass verge). You soon pass the entrance to Matley Wood campsite, and 80 paces further on is a broad track doubling sharply back on your right. The spire of Lyndhurst Church is just visible in the distance. This is the next option point.

Options

a) Follow the track parallel to the road — WALK 28A *(30 mins to Lyndhurst, 60 mins to Ashurst).*
b) Avoid the traffic — WALK 27 *(40 mins to Lyndhurst, 55 mins to Ashurst).*
c) Visit Matley Wood — WALK 16 *(80 mins to Lyndhurst, 50 mins to Ashurst).*

"The river bed has some unexpectedly deep pockets."

Walk 23

Face towards Lyndhurst, with the group of three silver birches on your right, and follow the road.

This is a quick route back to Lyndhurst along the road, suitable for the footsore but easier than the ridgeway path above.

Should you relent and wish to join the ridgeway after all there is a good track a little way along on the right which leads up to it.

Options

a) The Lyndhurst triangle — **WALK 1 and WALK 2** *(60 mins to Ashurst).*
b) Visit Lyndhurst and have some well earned refreshment before going home.

Walk 24

20 minutes

Compass Ref:25

Stand on the bridge, with the river flowing from left to right under you. Your track lies straight ahead, leading into some woodland after a short area of heath. Beware of taking tracks off to the left, especially when diverting round storm-felled trees.

This route is a continuation of the old SALT WAY (described in WALK 3) and has some attractive tree trunks by the path, with intermittent appearance of heath on both sides. Resist the temptation to deviate from the track for a quick kiss and cuddle; in summer the tall ferns give you a feeling of security, but every 10 to 15 minutes a family group is sure to pass by on some tiny track that is more effectively obscured by ferns than you.

Along this track, you will pass over what is in winter a vigorous stream. Unfortunately, just before this, the same stream returns the compliment by passing over your path and forcing you to jump it.

As you exit from this wood, a scrappy grass and heathland lies before you and you eventually reach a low wooden gate at a tarmac track. Stop here and select an option.

Options

a) You can see the pub dead ahead — WALK 25 *(75 mins to Lyndhurst, but only 10 mins to Ashurst).*

b) Turn back on WALK 24A *(55 mins to Lyndhurst, 60 mins to Ashurst).*

c) Turn right for a more extensive walk — WALK 15A *(70 mins to Lyndhurst, 70 mins to Ashurst).*

"The tall ferns give a feeling of security… but kids are sure to pass by."

Walk 25

10 minutes

Compass Ref:50

With the low Forestry access gate to your back, the tarmac road leads from Ashurst Lodge (to your right) to the main road (on your left). The pub, however, is visible ahead of you. Reach the green expanse by leaping the ditch and keep well away from the strip of wood on your right (mud lovers can keep closer in). Cross the tarmac road leading to the campsite, and take a small dirt track crossing the stream ahead, leading from the campsite to the road. Once over the bridge, those wanting the pub should make for the stile into its garden; those simply wanting Ashurst village should follow the track to the other stile by the road and turn right. A bus stop is thoughtfully provided for those too exhausted (or wet!) to return to Lyndhurst by any other route.

Options

a) Have a quick pint at one of the pubs in Ashurst.
b) Return to the "Access Limited" gate and choose **WALK 15A** *(70 mins to Lyndhurst),* or **WALK 24A** *(60 mins to Lyndhurst).*

Walk 26

A pleasant way to avoid the crowds. Face the green rectangle again and follow the path that comes down from behind you to keep to the outer (right-hand) border of the tall holly hedge — take this for a mere 60 paces and you will see a large wooden post at the gap in the hedge. You will also see through this gap in the hedge direct in front an even larger wooden post stuck in the middle of the grass. Turning your back on this second post, you will see two paths leading up into the trees. Toss a coin — if it lands heads, take the left fork, if it lands tails, go right. If the coin disappears in the undergrowth, it's not too late to take WALK 7.

These two paths form a complete circle, from the top of which a small track leads up over the heath. Follow this up to the slope. Do not stray to the left or you will become swallowed up in a boggy bottom, a rather thankless end after negotiating the Wicked Wet Wood.

This track has been laboriously paced out for us by the ponies, with a little help from the deer and the field mice. Ponies are notoriously fickle creatures, and occasionally whole groups will change their habits and desert existing tracks to create new ones — similar behaviour to that of Homo Sapiens when popularising trendy pubs, and then abandoning them just as suddenly.

Keep as straight a line as possible to the top of the slope (which is the ridgeway of WALK 2). The shifting line of pony tracks at the time of writing becomes less clear towards the top, but other walkers silhouetted against the skyline will show your direction. When you reach the ridgeway path, you are in the middle of WALK 2. Select an option.

Options

a) Turn right for Lyndhurst *(10 mins to Lyndhurst, 70 mins to Ashurst).*
b) Turn left to delve back into the Lyndhurst triangle — WALK 2 *(60 mins to Ashurst).*

Walk 27

Facing along the road away from Lyndhurst, the broad track slants off to your left. Twenty paces down this track, a small path comes off to the left to pass gently downhill through the woodland edging of gorse. Follow this little track which gradually widens out into attractive grassy turf.

The gorse and birch on your left finish, to reveal open heath for 50 paces. Just before the gorse border restarts, a small path appears on the left (indistinct as it comes off, but more obvious 20 paces further along). This path (WALK 5A) passes to the left of the band of gorse in the mid distance, and the spire of Lyndhurst Church can be seen in the far distance slightly to the right of the path.

If you want WALK 8, this point is not important; if you want WALK 5A, other tracks to the left will join up with the correct one should you miss it.

Options

a) Take the pony track across the moor — WALK 5A (*30 mins to Lyndhurst, 60 mins to Ashurst*).
b) Continue straight on — WALK 8 (*60 mins to Lyndhurst, 50 mins to Ashurst*).

Walk 28

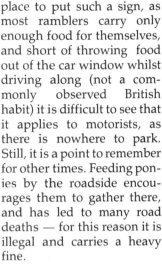

Compass Ref:100

Your walk starts from the three silver birches growing together, and you should follow the direction of the road away from Lyndhurst, (you can keep off the hard stuff by walking on the remains of the old road, a broad green strip of turf several paces to the left).

There is a young pine inclosure blocking the view on your right, but the superb panorama on your left more than makes up for it.

After a short while you pass a sign warning you not to feed the ponies; it is an odd place to put such a sign, as most ramblers carry only enough food for themselves, and short of throwing food out of the car window whilst driving along (not a commonly observed British habit) it is difficult to see that it applies to motorists, as there is nowhere to park. Still, it is a point to remember for other times. Feeding ponies by the roadside encourages them to gather there, and has led to many road deaths — for this reason it is illegal and carries a heavy fine.

About 100 paces past this sign. the edge of Matley Wood begins on the left, and a broad track forks off left. You can now choose your next option. (If you reach the entrance to Matley Wood campsite, you have gone 80 paces too far).

Options

a) Follow the road straight on to the pub at Beaulieu Road — WALK 22A *(110 mins to Lyndhurst, 100 mins to Ashurst).*
b) Take the broad track left for a younger wood leading to a wide range of scenery — WALK 16 *(80 mins to Lyndhurst, 50 mins to Ashurst).*
c) Take the smaller track forking off left from the broader track to follow the edge of Matley Wood — WALK 27 *(40 mins to Lyndhurst, 55 mins to Ashurst).*

Walk 1 A

Straight ahead of you is the town of Lyndhurst, easily recognised by its tall church spire. A hundred years ago, John Wise (THE NEW FOREST) wrote that "the people of Lyndhurst ought, I always think, to be the happiest and most contented in England" — and perhaps they should, being surrounded literally on all sides by open forest and heath. Today, most of the buildings have a distinctly Victorian look, but occupation can be traced back as far as the Iron Age, proving that the locals know a good spot when they see one. But Lyndhurst's popularity has meant that there is progressively less room for all its visitors. The wild ponies were the first to go, finally seen off the streets a few years back. Maybe the cars will be next in line, now that the bypass looks more than just a distant promise.

Options

a) WALK 1 — *(65 mins to Ashurst).*

Looking down to Bolton's Bench car park (Walk 1A)

Cemetery Chapel, Bolton's Bench

Walk 2A

You can see the spire of Lyndhurst Church in the distance, and the imposing residence of Northerwood House on the hill to its right. Make along this broad ridgeway track.

Although the track leads you directly to Lyndhurst, it is worth avoiding the crowds by taking any of the short paths off on the left after you have climbed the slope. As you break through the gorse, turn right and follow the narrow track(s) along the slope, with open grass and heather to your left, looking down to the road, and the gorse bushes to your right (you may get swallowed up in the ferns in the height of summer).

You are now doing your bit to erode the remains of a medieval deer enclosure, by walking along its raised boundary. Still, it will probably survive a few more visitors, having been built in 1299. Perhaps you could carry an anti-bloodsports banner to compensate for any damage caused.

Keeping to the right and avoiding going down the slope, you will eventually come to an odd-shaped concrete block, which is a "Trigpoint". Here it is necessary to turn right to regain the main path.

If you have children with you, let them gather the scented flowers of the many gorse bushes around here. These flowers were traditionally thrown in the water when boiling eggs for Easter, giving them a bright yellow tint. Try it!

Options

a) Join your car, or drop into Lyndhurst first for some refreshment.
b) Turn back to Ashurst — WALK 2 *(60 mins to Ashurst).*

Walk 3A

The initial path is a little unclear, especially if muddy. Stand on the bridge, with the stream running from right to left, and walk straight ahead. As you pass through the first few trees, you will see the path leading uphill to the ridge top. A clump of firs on a hill can be seen bordering the right of the path in the mid distance. As you approach these firs, the mud decreases and you say good-bye to the bog on your left.

You arc now following the SALT WAY, an important route for the transport of salt into the country from Lymington in the old days. No doubt it was much used by 18th century smugglers, too. Smuggling makes most people think of brandy in oaken casks, and boxes of baccy, but in fact the main trade was in tea. English tastes have changed little over the years, and many a life was lost in the illicit tea trade until the duty was substantially reduced in 1745. It is estimated that 3 million pounds (weight) were smuggled in, making three out of every four cuppas illegal. The stakes were high — at one trial, it was revealed that a night's work could net each man half-a-guinea, a horse, and free food and drink. On top of this, he would receive the proceeds of a 'dollop' of tea; a 'dollop' was a half bag weighing 13 lbs. and fetching about 25 shillings. All this in the days when an honest day's labour would earn you 17 pence. For the benefit of readers unfamiliar with the £.s.d. of the good old days, my reckoning suggests that one night's smuggling was equivalent to about 6 weeks of ordinary labouring work.

The bog on your right remains much in evidence before the firs half-way up the hill. The highest point of the scrub in this bog was called Row Hill; it was the target area for the Rifle Volunteers, giving a range of 900 yards in a straight line from Lyndhurst village. Perhaps they sometimes used the smugglers as target practice?

As you reach the top of the slope the path runs into a T-junction with the ridgeway path. A few other paths also start at this important junction. The choice is yours!

Options

a) Turn right to Lyndhurst — WALK 2A *(15 mins to Lyndhurst, 75 mins to Ashurst).*
b) Further exploration of the Lyndhurst triangle? — WALK 5 *(45 mins to Lyndhurst, 70 mins to Ashurst).*
c) A short walk to the road? WALK 4 *(35 mins to Lyndhurst, 70 mins to Ashurst).*

Walk 4A

8 minutes

Compass Ref:300

At the three silver birches joined together on the right-hand side of the road facing Lyndhurst, a broad track leads gently off to the right into the gorse and heather.

met by a wide path coming up from the right and a small pony track across the moorland is between this and you. Yet another path can be seen on your left.

Walk 4A

You will soon confirm you are on the right track because the number of tourists increases dramatically. (Why is it that when exploring new places everybody else is a tourist, but never you?)

As the path leads gently downhill and bends to the left, the main ridgeway path (for this is what you are on) is

Options

a) Lyndhurst and some welcome refreshments — keep on the main path by selecting **WALK 2A** *(15 mins to Lyndhurst, 75 mins to Ashurst).*
b) Take the main path on the right for the promised land — **WALK 3** *(60 mins to Lyndhurst, 45 mins to Ashurst).*
c) Fancy a pony track across the moor, leading to an interesting wood? **WALK 5** *(45 mins to Lyndhurst, 70 mins to Ashurst).*

Walk 5A

A lovely walk this, along a track made for ponies, not people. Standing on the main track, with the wood 200 paces behind you, a small track gradually forms across the heath (the first few paces are difficult to make out). Lyndhurst church steeple is clearly visible in the distance just to the right of the track. If you are in the right spot, the path should pass to the left of a thicket of gorse in the mid-distance. It doesn't matter if you choose the wrong track, as long as it points towards the steeple, for they all end up in the same place.

Towards the end of this path you will often come across a small group of donkeys. Not all donkeys are as morose as Eeyore — in fact they often welcome a bit of company. However, they are very protective of their young, and will attack you if you get too close to their foals — content yourself with taking photos. Also, remember that dogs and donkeys do not mix. A frisky dog is likely to make a donkey panic, and emit a high-pitched bray — dogs tend to think that this is great fun, which makes them become even more provocative. The tables are turned during the foaling season when donkeys will leave off their grazing for the pleasure of tossing any dog passing within 30 paces. Beware!

You will eventually come up to the broad ridgeway path, with another broad path going fairly steeply down to the river on your right. At this junction, you have some further options to take, and you will be relieved to know that you are no longer forced to keep to single file.

Options

a) **Turn right to visit the Beaulieu river — WALK 3** *(60 mins to Lyndhurst, 45 mins to Ashurst).*
b) **Join the main ridgeway path straight ahead — WALK 2A** *(15 mins to Lyndhurst, 75 mins to Ashurst).*
c) **A short walk up to the road? WALK 4** *(35 mins to Lyndhurst, 70 mins to Ashurst).*

WALKS 6A and 7A

These walks are designed in the other direction only.

Walk 8A

With Matley Wood on your left, take the track gradually leaving the wood dead ahead.

In the same way that Mother Nature ensures that dock leaves always grow close by a nettle patch, so she ensures that in the Forest wherever there is a fly, there groweth a fly-swat. Accordingly, bracken is to be found in great abundance along this woodland edge. Before reaching to select one of these ferns as your fly-swat, bear in mind the following points — (i) low down the leaf-stalk is sharp and stringy, i.e. they fight back (ii) lower down still an adder may be lurking, already feeling disgruntled that you have disturbed his sunbathing. (I generally reckon to meet one adder per 200 miles of Forest walking), (iii) you may pull up a wild gladiolus by mistake. There are a few remaining bracken-covered woodland edges where these flowers are still to be found and this is reputedly one of them. They are extinct elsewhere in Britain.

Bracken is a furious grower — one day you will see the first few "shepherds's crooks" as its young shoots break through last year's debris, and within 3 or 4 weeks it is standing five feet tall. In autumn, its glorious colours enrich the Forest, and as it darkens and collapses, it provides a protective canopy beneath which other plants and small animals spend their winter. By the time spring comes around, the bracken is mostly flattened out — and from here, the empty casings of last year's Giant Puffballs roll out and blow about the landscape like enormous dessicated buns. Starting life in summer as solid, fleshy balls of fungus, they burst open and release their spores in autumn; and the only parts still living in winter-time are fine white strands enjoying a communal "mould-in" with all the other fungi on the Forest floor.

After a short while, the track bends to the left and a path strikes off on the right across the heathland. The grass broadens out so much here as it curves left that it is difficult to make out the track but you will see that it follows the line of the wood 200 paces on your left. As you go uphill, two or three narrow paths leave the main track on the right, pointing to Lyndhurst church spire in the distance. These are all difficult to see until you have covered the first few yards, after which they become obvious. Stop here to select your next option.

Options

a) Continue uphill to the road — **WALK 27A** *(35 mins to Lyndhurst, 60 mins to Ashurst).*
b) Turn right to follow a delightful pony track across the heath — **WALK 5A** *(30 mins to Lyndhurst, 60 mins to Ashurst).*

Walk 8A

Walk 9A

A naturalist's delight. Follow the broad, often muddy track round the lower edge of Matley Wood. The thin strip of wood on the right abounds in mushrooms and toadstools amongst the ferns. The woodland edge is abruptly cut off by sloping boggy heathland.

In five minutes, at the right time of year, one could fill a carrier bag with the edible Boletus mushroom, although the Forestry Commission may frown on this (cropping blackberries in autumn is generally regarded as fair game, taking anything else is poaching). The Boletus is the main ingredient of many commercial 'mushroom' soups, but I must confess that my family were not unduly impressed by my attempts to soup them. Grilled or fried though, they are superb. However, NEVER eat any fungus you are not 100% sure is completely safe — a few fatalities occur every year, when families gather a number of look-alikes in a wood that turn out not to be taste-alikes.

Just as the view opens out on the right, a broad track crosses yours from out of the wood on your left, and strikes off down the heath on your right. Time already for another option.

Options

a) **Straight on along the woodland fringe — WALK 8A** *(40 mins to Lyndhurst, 60 mins to Ashurst).*

b) **A quick route down to the river — WALK 14** *(50 mins to Lyndhurst, 40 mins to Ashurst).*

Heathland by Matley Wood (Walk 14)

Walk 10 A

This route follows the right-hand fork (as you face uphill), with heathland on the left and a good example of bog-land on your right.

Local people hereabouts — whom you are likely to meet on your rambles — are remarkably tolerant of strangers, considering some of the things which have been written about them in the past. Hudson's comments (Hampshire Days, 1903) are typical, referring to them as "parasites of the Forest." John Gilpin (rector of Boldre Church in the late 18th century) declares that "the Forester, who has the temptation of plunder on every side, finds it easier to trespass than to work, and becomes a supple, crafty, pilfering knave." He then details the habits of the forestry labourers (then called "undertakers") whom he held responsible for the failure of several attempts to replant the ravaged Forest in these years. The undertakers had a right to cut holly and underwood of little value to browze the deer; they would subsequently sell the dried sticks as faggots. However, this right was often abused by the indiscriminate thinning out of the best, rather than the weakest, saplings and 'accidentally' cutting down branches two feet thick from mature trees. Gilpin held the common day-labourers in even lower esteem, suspecting them of widespread poaching. He also failed to admire their skill in removing entire trees overnight!

Today, the most roguish locals seem content to pull the leg of the inquisitive outsiders, with tales of the old treacle mines deep in the heart of the Forest, and how smugglers from overseas would sail in to exchange their illicit goods for that highly prized commodity.

As you enter the wood, continue another 60 paces to reach a poorly defined crossroads, ignoring 2 forks to the right before this that lead to WALK 9A. Select your option.

Options

a) **Turn right to follow the attractive woodland edge —** WALK 9A *(45 mins to Lyndhurst, 50 mins to Ashurst).*
b) **Turn left to follow the woodland edge the other way. A clearer path may be found 40 paces on if preferred — they soon join up. WALK 17** *(50 mins to Lyndhurst, 50 mins to Ashurst).*

Walk 11A

Cross over the bridge (with the water running from right to left) to follow the broad track uphill. Just after the river, on the left, is a large mound which in summer is covered in ferns. It is one of the largest tumuli in the Forest — so fascinating to the Victorians, but quite unnoticed today (perhaps because grave robbing has gone out of style).

You may have pondered the singular lack of two popular grazing animals in the Forest — goats and sheep. Goats are actually barred, on account of their destructive grazing habits, but sheep are just too silly to succeed. They have been tried in the past, but like my mother-in-law, they have very short legs, and will insist on venturing into the bogs, from which they find it impossible to escape.

Take the path up the hill, with an excellent bog on your right. When the path forks as it levels out, you take your next option.

Options

a) The woodland fringe — fork right on WALK 10A *(50 mins to Lyndhurst, 55 mins to Ashurst).*
b) The heart of Matley Wood, or an extended walk across the plains to Beaulieu Road — WALK 18 *(55 mins to Lyndhurst, 55 mins to Ashurst).*

Walk 12A

Face the bridge, with the water flowing from left to right. Cross over and turn right to follow the left bank of the Beaulieu River downstream.

Keep to the grassy strip with the river on your right. This is a continuation of the Longwater Lawn, but the heath on the left is doing its best to overrun it. You will soon reach a drainage ditch entering from your left, identifiable by its straightness, which is quite incompatible with the surrounding scene. I shall leave you to find a way across as an initiative test. AFTER you have found it, you may care to read WALK 12 to see how the folks in the other direction approached the problem.

The turf here is frequently water-logged, being so close to the river that at times it is hard to distinguish between the two. This section is very rich in wild-life; if you are not too busy keeping dry underfoot, take a little time to search it out. The river itself is for the most part hard to reach because of a thorny cloak of brambles and dog-rose scrambling amongst the alder and willow trees. This protective screen provides shelter for all sorts of creatures. Damsel flies buzz round you in the summer, flashing their electric blue bodies, and many other insect species thrive in the damp conditions. In their wake can be seen all sorts of birds, from delicate robins, warblers and wrens, to sturdy ducks and pheasants. Weasels, badgers, foxes and hedgehogs are also present — but you'll have to get past those thorns to see them. You soon reach the next bridge over the river (not over the ditch) and have to choose an option.

Options

a) Turn left onto WALK 15A (*75 mins to Lyndhurst, 30 mins to Ashurst*).
b) Turn right for woodland or extensive plains — WALK 11A (*55 mins to Lyndhurst, 60 mins to Ashurst*).

The Beaulieu River (Walk 12A)

Standing on the bridge with the river flowing from left to right under you, cross over and turn left to follow the river bank. The coppice soon gives way to open ground and the beautiful twists and turns of the river's lazy journey are revealed.

Keep close to the bank. Those fit enough may care to leap the river to examine an interesting pond almost hidden from view on the other side.

Visitors whose roots are firmly in the town may perhaps be feeling nervous of some of the beasts on this plain. Let me put your mind at rest at once: not one of these animals will harm you in any way, provided you appreciate that they are wild animals and respect their independence. A distance of 10 paces from them is safe at all times unless they have very young animals at heel, when it is wiser to keep a little further away, taking care not to place yourself between the mother and offspring. New Forest ponies have been selected by man and nature for their hardiness and self-reliance. Geneticists have noted that these chromosomal traits are inversely linked with a predisposition to congeniality. Put another way, these ponies have no sense of humour at all. A pony may deign to let you fondle it and pat its neck, but the next moment is likely to bite or kick you. So leave them well alone, and you can relax and admire their beauty.

Young cows have a naturally curious nature and will occasionally approach you to investigate; they are merely desiring a good look and a sniff. They will never bite you — the worst they will do is to give you a lick. Even this is unlikely, since they are much more frightened of you than you are of them. Any males you may meet in the Forest will be of a gentle

persuasion, and will have had a little operation to keep them that way.

Donkeys, for most of the year the most affectionate of our Forest beasts, should not be approached within 20 paces when with their very young, especially if you have a dog.

Continuing along the river, you will soon arrive at the next bridge. It has a small, solitary oak tree on one side to keep it company, and the old Parish Boundary stones on the other. It is a rare person who does not wish to tarry a while at this delightful spot. However, you will eventually have to rise to choose another option.

Options

a) **The sane man's return to Lyndhurst — WALK 3A** *(40 mins to Lyndhurst, 70 mins to Ashurst).*

b) **Feeling mad? WALK 6** *(30 mins to Lyndhurst if all goes well, 70 mins to Ashurst).*

c) **Extend your walk through the wood — WALK 24** *(100 mins to Lyndhurst, 40 mins to Ashurst).*

Cross over the bridge (with the stream flowing from right to left) and head uphill (ignoring the other track slightly to the right).

Bridge over the Beaulieu River (Walk 14A)

This is an easy straight track up to Matley Wood. In summer, your walking on this path will contribute to the death and destruction of a plant that is all but extinct elsewhere in Britain. Lift up your left foot and observe what is under it. You are now viewing the crushed remains of a Sundew, its little red rosette of leaves no longer glistening with an enticing sticky dew. Did you destroy its flower-head too — those pretty white flowers that were on top of a long stalk? Ah well — comfort yourself with the knowledge that this is the Dr. Death of the English plant world. Many an innocent insect has been lured onto its attractive tentacles, to become stuck fast and await its turn on the Sundew's dinner menu. Still we of the flesh often eat plants — why shouldn't

some plants turn the tables? Both the round-leaved species and the pear-leafed species exist around here, but just to confuse you, they do quite a lot of interbreeding, so intermediate forms can also be found. Not, however, during the winter — the Sundew sprouts from seed only when the danger of frost is over.

A few paces into the wood will bring you to a crossroads, (the track to the right is initially unclear, being very broad and grassy). Pause here to select your next option.

Options

a) Turn left for a choice of extensive routes — WALK 9 *(65 mins to Lyndhurst, 40 mins to Ashurst).*

b) Turn right along the woodland fringe to the heath — WALK 8A *(40 mins to Lyndhurst, 70 mins to Ashurst).*

Deer are common in the New Forest and easier to find
than many people realise.

Walk 15A

Follow the tarmac track away from the main road, and you will shortly notice a watertrough in the middle of the heather on your right. Continue up the tarmac track.

This is one area of remaining Forest dubbed "Ancient and Ornamental Woodland", which is a grand way of saying that we have so far resisted the temptation to modernise it. Actually, of course, there is no such thing in Britain as "natural" woodland; even this wood has always been managed to some extent. Its blend of open spaces and ancient trees is the direct result of the type of management practised from Norman to mediaeval times: to create a new wood in the same style today would take more than 300 years. Even the word "Forest" has changed its meaning over the centuries. To most people, it signifies a "large wood", but it referred originally to large tracts of open countryside with woods dotted around here and there — the whole area being purposely kept that way for the King's hunting. A typical Forest scene was lush green pastureland with a few tall trees scattered about, and areas of coppice undergrowth — hazel, holly, hawthorn, birch and blackthorn. This undergrowth was kept to a manageable size by regu-

larly chopping the tops off at head height ("pollarding"); a run-down area would be encoppiced for a few years by enclosing it with a fence or a hedge along a raised bank to keep out browsing deer, horses and cattle.

By and large, the nobility and the peasants lived here in reasonable harmony; the former had their hunting, and the latter had their produce (and the poaching). It was only in the late mediaeval times that conflict built up, as the nobility began to lose interest in hunting and turned to building large timber houses and ships instead. Many oaks were felled and removed for the sake of this new interest, and few were replaced. The old practice of pollarding was found to take up too much space, so in 1698 it was

stopped altogether. Thus the grand old oaks and beeches you see about you, with branches spreading out just above head height, are mostly between 300 and 500 years old. (Pollarding also had the happy effect of extending the life of a tree.)

In the 19th century, a growing demand for attractive recreational areas led to a ban on all new inclosures in 1877. Clearly the results of the inclosure system were not understood, and Nature was believed to have produced these woods all on her own. The 1877 Act still forms the broad foundation for current management of the New Forest, sometimes handicapping rather than helping the work of the Forestry Commission. The Commission has to maintain a balance among all the different demands made on the Forest: to produce timber economically, to provide adequate grazing for Commoners' stock, to ensure that unique habitats are protected and to allow ample access for recreation.

As you approach the entrance to Ashurst Lodge, turn right by a leafy glade and follow the fence which encloses the Lodge grounds. The path leads downhill to a bridge over the young Beaulieu river, where you must choose your next option.

Options

a) Follow the river upstream — WALK 12 *(55 mins to Lyndhurst, 50 mins to Ashurst).*
b) Strike up to Matley Wood on WALK 11A *(55 mins to Lyndhurst, 60 mins to Ashurst).*

Walk 16A

At this cross-roads, stand so that the grassy plain (behind the flimsy line of gorse) is on your left. Take the broad path straight ahead into the woods, ignoring tracks off the heath to the right or the left.

Matley Wood has never been an official inclosure, at least in recent centuries, although some ancient banks suggest it was once enclosed. Its lower slopes extend gradually downhill from the South, taking over from heathland and demonstrating in classical textbook fashion how grassland in suitable areas eventually becomes forest.(WALKS 8 and 9 on the wood's fringes, are beautiful illustrations of the process).

An INCLOSURE, incidentally, is an area set aside by Act of Parliament for the purpose of excluding deer and commoners' animals in order to grow trees. Inclosures have a formal arrangement of trees planted by man (especially the pine inclosures of recent times), often with long runs of straight drainage ditches and a fenced boundary giving an abrupt end to the tree line. The more ancient an inclosure, the more run-down the boundary becomes, often showing only as a moss covered bank separating a deteriorating formality from the more informal clumps of self-sown trees beyond. Prior to the inclosures, which began on a modest scale in 1669. areas were fenced off or hedged for a few years to enable natural regeneration to take place free from browsing animals. But the ground was never cleared first, and the boundaries often took on very erratic shapes as they tried to include valuable old trees.

Most of the trees here in Matley Wood are 100 to 200 years old and appear to have been planted by man. They have been mysteriously protected from grazing animals when young, despite no legal right to enclose the wood — a quiet piece of private enterprise from Denny Lodge perhaps? Note the handsome hollies abounding amongst the chestnuts and oaks. Most holly trees in the Forest are gnarled and twisted into ancient forms, or are struggling for survival as tiny scrubby bushes. Here they are tall and standing proudly amongst their grander neighbours. The bare trunk below about 5 foot is not, however, entirely natural — left to its own devices, a holly tree would modestly hide its trunk right down to the ground, but in winter browsing deer and ponies will strip the lower leaves and branches for food. The tendency for deer in a hard winter to strip the bark also, sometimes even killing the tree, probably accounts for the twisted shapes of other Forest hollies on the woodland fringes; perhaps here some magic spirit afforded them a degree of protection in their youth.

After labouring uphill for a while you come to a low Forestry access gate. Continue STRAIGHT ON. Do not deviate into the campsite. This camp entrance track curves left 40 paces before the road, but you should ignore the curve and take the old original track straight on to the road. You can now take your next option.

Options

a) **Turn sharp left towards Beaulieu Road Station —** **WALK 22A** *(110 mins to Lyndhurst, 100 mins to Ashurst).*
b) **Turn sharp right down the narrow track along the woodland edge — WALK 27** *(35 mins to Lyndhurst, 55 mins to Ashurst).*
c) **Follow the road ahead — WALK 28A** *(30 mins to Lyndhurst, 60 mins to Ashurst).*

Entrance to Matley Wood from the road

Walk 17A

At this cross-roads, stand so that the grassy plain (behind the flimsy line of gorse) is on your left; on your right is a good path stretching down over the heath with a wood on its right in the distance. Take the path ahead, but instead of continuing directly into the wood, turn right at the cross-roads 170 paces on. This track passes through a short strip of gorse onto the edge of Matley Wood.

It was in this area that my wife and I spent the best part of a moonlit night one early summer (although the air temperature was more like mid-winter) waiting to view Mother Badger with her playful brood. I should like to pass some of my experience of badger watching on to you — (i) always take a comfortable chair with you (this we did) (ii) always wear ear muffs (this we didn't do), else the sound of falling leaves in the dead of night will make you wonder if you are in the middle of an SAS night exercise (iii) always check beforehand that you are actually sitting by a badger sett (this we took great care to do) (iv) never mistake some glistening moist moss on an overhanging root for badger droppings, assuming you have thus found evidence of an active badger sett (this we lamentably failed to do!). If you take this advice you will not be so likely to follow our example of a fruitless night spent watching a disused rabbit hole.

Shortly after you enter the fringe of the wood, you come to a broad path leading out of the wood on the left and running down over the heath.

Options

a) Carry straight across the "coming-out-of-the-wood-path", and continue along the attractive woodland fringe — **WALK 9A** *(45 mins to Lyndhurst, 50 mins to Ashurst)*.
b) Turn right to follow the heath down to the river — **WALK 10** *(55 mins to Lyndhurst, 30 mins to Ashurst)*.

Walk 18A

At this cross-roads, turn your back to the grassy plain (behind the flimsy line of gorse): straight ahead is a good path stretching down over the heath with a wood on its right in the distance. Take this path, which is easy all the way except for a small stretch at the beginning which threatens to envelop you in mud.

This is only a short link-route, but there is an interesting bog and tumulus on your left as you lead off.

A path merges with yours at a sharp angle from the left and you are back to choosing an option already.

Options

a) Carry on downhill — WALK **11** (*60 mins to Lyndhurst, 35 mins to Ashurst*).

b) Changed your mind, and want the woodland fringe after all? Turn sharp left onto WALK **10A** (*50 mins to Lyndhurst, 55 mins to Ashurst*).

Walk 19A

30 minutes

Compass Ref:5

Walk 19A

A rewarding walk across some fine open country. Cross the road from Shatterford Bottom car park, and follow the broad track as it keeps the railway on its right. After the path steepens its descent, you come out to a wide, grassy plain — also known locally as a "lawn".

On the opposite side of this plain is a line of trees protecting a river. There is no distinct path, but you should cross the plain and head for an imaginary gap halfway along the line of trees. As you get close, the path reappears.

The ponies you see about you are still very much in the wild state — a fact which is dramatically illustrated during a pony round-up. As a child, I remember mingling with a group of people close by this very spot, and hearing the thunder of many hooves in the distance. Then, in true Wild West style, a multitude of wild horses appeared from over the brow, skillfully contained by

three men on horseback, one at the rear, and one on each flank. Amidst much noise and excitement, they were coralled onto one of the old

railway bridges. Then the foals were branded and sorted for sale. The chaos appeared overwhelming to an outsider, but a good day's work emerged from all the bustle. Less dramatic methods have been employed, such as bribing those grazing by the road with bread and quickly lassooing them with a rope anchored to a sturdy vehicle. But now that roadside feeding is forbidden (because of the danger of accidents) the ponies are not so easily fooled.

On the far side of the lawn, you will reach the King's Passage. Cross over both bridges, keeping a tight hold of your dog (the mud here is rich in hydrogen sulphide gas of rotten eggs fame). As you exit from the passage, a second plain, Matley Holms, will be revealed.

Although the ponies live wild, they do actually belong to individual commoners, i.e. with Right of Common of Pasture. Each commoner has his own brand for you to spot on the pony (several local pubs display the full range of those used). During the autumn roundups, the foals are branded with the same iron used previously on their

Beaulie Road Pony Sale

mare. Any pony to be turned out again also has a hair-cut — the tail is clipped as an indication that the annual fee (currently £10.00) has been paid to the Agister. There are four Agisters, a unique form of 'Forest Policeman' each responsible for one section of the Forest. The walks described in this book are all within the No.3 District, where the ponies have a double tail trim on the right-hand side. They look very smart in the autumn and winter, but by summer the clip marks become difficult to spot. You may also notice quite a few with the entire outer ring of hair clipped out half-way up the tail — these are interlopers from No.1 District, making a raid on this tasty lawn. The railway marks the border between the districts, and "immigration controls" on the railway bridges are noticeably lax.

Walk straight across to the opposite side of Matley Holms until you reach the heather and gorse. Pay attention to the navigating here, or else you will pick up the wrong trail. Follow the gorse fringe along on its left; 60 paces before the border of the plain turns left is a path which breaks through the gorse on your right to cross the heath. Take this. Twenty paces on, a broader path crosses yours and you are at your next option point. You

should be facing a path which runs straight ahead over the heath with some woodland to the right of it in the mid distance.

Options

a) Straight ahead over the heath to the river — WALK 18A *(65 mins to Lyndhurst, 40 mins to Ashurst).*
b) Want to visit the heart of Matley Wood? — turn left onto WALK 16A *(45 mins to Lyndhurst, 40 mins to Ashurst).*
c) Prefer the woodland fringe? — turn left (sharing the first bit with 16A) onto WALK 17A *(55 mins to Lyndhurst, 45 mins to Ashurst).*

The Woods Pass ... (Walk 18A)

Walk 20A

SILVA®

A road walk primarily for those desperate to reach the pub before closing time. With the tarmac track to Denny Wood on your right, strike off down the road, keeping on the right-hand verge till you reach Shatterford car park just before the railway bridge.

I assume you are either footsore or unusually thirsty to have selected this route — tarmac walking is somewhat dull, although the type of driving met along here will perhaps raise your adrenalin a little. A hundred years ago this stretch of road was described as bearing "comparison as a bad road with any in the Sahara". Unless the author was run down by a camel train, I assume he was referring to its wild unmade-up state. Personally I would have been happy if it had been left that way.

Some inconsiderate builder of tumuli in Roman times has seriously obscured your view to the left, but extensive views over one of our most treacherous bogs, Shatterford Bottom, can be enjoyed on the right.

Options

a) Over the bridge to the pub *(return to the car park for next option).*
b) WALK 21 for open woodland past some attractive heath *(75 mins to Lyndhurst, 100 mins to Ashurst).*
c) Left onto WALK 19A for classic New Forest plains *(70 mins to Lyndhurst, 65 mins to Ashurst).*

Walk 21A

A highly attractive route, with a mixture of fine ancient oak/beech woodland and heath. However, in this direction the track through the wood requires a little initiative.

Follow the tarmac track through the Denny Wood camp-site. Ignore the forestry access gate on the left just past the 2nd water/ waste disposal point, take the next gate left, having continued some way along the road before it enters Denny Lodge territory. By the gate is the carcass of an ancient beech which died despite re-pollarding in 1985.

"Pollarding", or chopping the tops of trees off at head height to make it easier to gather the branches, has not (legally!) been practised in the Forest since 1698. In that year, King William (of William 'n' Mary fame) who was never a great deer hunter, forbade pollarding in order to promote the growth of quality timber in long lengths, for ship-building. In the interest of history, I have shinned up this newly-pollarded tree and counted the exposed rings of the main trunk. To my surprise, the ring-count was 190 on each severed bough – proving that the tree was still being pollarded for about 100 years after the practice became illegal! My guess is that branches were persuaded to fall off accidentally every few years – the evidence would be gone by morning, and only those who know the wood intimately (ie. the miscreants themselves) would miss the loss of a single bough.

Follow the track through the wood; if it becomes indistinct at times, do not worry – woodland is very open and dry here. BUT YOU MUST KEEP THE EDGE OF THE BOGGY HEATH ON YOUR LEFT MORE OR LESS IN VIEW AT ALL TIMES.

This section of wood is one of the most beautiful in the Forest. It used to be called the "Cathedral Beeches" because of the graceful arches formed by the trees along your way. These beeches survived the chop when Denny Wood Inclosure was formed in 1860, encompassing many older inclosures and ancient woodland, but many were damaged during the drought in 1976, and the storms of 1988 and 1990 were the last straw. Few had been pollarded (which greatly extends their life), so perhaps Nature was calling them in anyway.

When you come across a track which points out of the wood to the left, take it. It becomes a good wide path as it leaves the wood and heads for Beaulieu Road

station. There are actually two paths doing this – they join up by a clump of silver birches outside the wood, so you have a double chance of success.

The track passes, by way of a wooden bridge, over Shatterford Bottom; this is one of the most impenetrable bogs in the Forest, as shown by the white tufts of Cotton Grass. Together with Matley Bog and Stephill Bottom, it forms a circle round Beaulieu Road station, and under no circumstances should be crossed other than by the official passages marked on an Ordnance Survey map.

You eventually pass through a loose-knit group of pines to reach Shatterford car-park, and after popping over the railway bridge for a well-earned pint, return here to select another option.

Options

a) You had more than one pint at the Beaulieu Hotel and now think it might be easier to walk back along the road? WALK 20 *(60 mins to Lyndhurst, 85 mins to Ashurst).*
b) Cross the road to some fine grassland plains — WALK 19A *(70 mins to Lyndhurst, 65 mins to Ashurst).*

Walk 22A

Facing away from Lynd-hurst, with woodland on both sides, follow the road along, past the entrance to Matley Wood camp-site and turn in the next left-hand track which leads you through a car park.

Just before the tarmac turns into a car park, you will see a sign on the left with the message **"PLEASE TAKE YOUR LITTER HOME"**. I have yet to meet a pig suffi-ciently literate to read and follow this request, but it is presumably a hangover from the days when Matley Wood was visited by pigs during the "pannage season". This is in the autumn, when those Forest small-holdings with Rights of Pannage can release their pigs to gobble up the "mast" (i.e. the fallen fruits of the Forest). The favourite and most abundant such fruit is the acorn, but beechnuts and sweet chest-nuts are both included. There are plenty of sweet chestnuts in Matley Wood (unusually for the Forest), but pannage has not been practised here in recent times. Fritham is one of the few Forest hamlets where it still takes place. Not only does pannage help to produce fine pork, it also clears the ground of acorns — which, if eaten in large quantities by cattle and (especially) horses, are toxic and even occasionally fatal. But this applies to green acorns: by the time they turn brown, they are highly nutri-tious to both deer and cattle, so the poor pigs are ordered

out of the Forest once more. Nevertheless, pannage was considered very important in olden times — the Domesday Book records the value of woodland in terms of its available pannage, not its timber-content.

Now cross over the little stream (a tributary of the young Beaulieu River), and reach the main road continuing in the same direction; as the road bends sharp left there is a little tarmac track straight ahead which serves as an entrance to Denny Wood camp-site and as an escape route for those drivers who didn't realise there was a bend just here. Stop to take your next option.

Options

a) Continue on the road ahead — WALK 20A *(90 mins to Lyndhurst, 85 mins to Ashurst).*
b) Bear right for attractive woodland and heath — WALK 21A *(95 mins to Lyndhurst, 100 mins to Ashurst).*

WALK 23A

This walk is designed in the other direction only.

Walk 24A

Walk 24A

Cross over the low Forestry access gate to follow the broad track over a short strip of heath into the wood.

This is a continuation of the old SALT WAY of WALK 3 and you will pass several attractive trees by the path, with intermittent appearance of heath on either or both sides. You are now on the edge of an 'Ancient and Ornamental Woodland'. The area was probably largely pastureland in medieval times, with a light cover of oaks and beech. Now abandoned to its own devices, a battle is taking place between the advancing heath on your left and the dense woodland on your right. Self-sown Silver Birches combine with bracken and brambles to give a protective cover in which acorns can sprout; and as you go deeper into the woods, you will see these young oak saplings getting progressively grander. They are all of one type — the Pedunculate Oak. Our other similar oak, the Sessile Oak, has much greater difficulty in self-sowing, and is rare around here. "What's with this sessile and pedunculate?" I hear you say. Well, 'peduncle' means stalk, and 'sessile' means without a stalk, so the Pedunculate Oak has an acorn on a stalk,

moment to investigate the deeper wood on your right — not an oak in sight! A dense forest of mature beech and barely enough light for anything else. Three hundred years ago, the Forest was stripped of most of the oaks which were accessible to the road, to form His Majesty's fleet (the picturesque bends in an oak were ideal material for some of the knotty woodwork problems). Left to themselves, the beech have flourished, and only the advancing woodland edge of self-sown oaks reveals this was once a mixed beech and oak forest. What stories these woods may tell if we have eyes to see.

As you exit from this wood, a bridge over the young Beaulieu River is before you across the heath. Stop at this bridge.

and the Sessile Oak has an acorn without a stalk. If it's the wrong time of year for acorns look at the leaves: the Pedunculate Oak has a leaf with *no* stalk, the Sessile Oak has a leaf *with* a stalk. Award yourself ten marks if by the end of this walk you can remember that the Pedunculate Oak has a stalky acorn with a stalkless leaf, and the Sessile Oak vice versa (or was it the other way round...?).

As you walk along this track, you pass through three hundred years of time; the woodland fringe has grown up into a mature oak forest. But just leave the path for a

Options

a) Continue the old Salt Way uphill, the easy route to Lyndhurst — WALK 3A (35 mins to Lyndhurst, 55 mins to Ashurst).

b) Turn left for a beautiful stroll along the river — WALK 13 (60 mins to Lyndhurst, 55 mins to Ashurst).

c) Turn right to the Wicked Wet Wood if you dare! WALK 6 (35 mins to Lyndhurst with luck, 70 mins to Ashurst).

Walk 25A

This walk is intended for those who have started out from Ashurst, but will also prove useful for those from Lyndhurst who have memory problems related to over-indulgence in the pub.

Starting from either the road stile or the New Forest Hotel garden stile, cross the little stream by way of the dirt track, and make direct for the gravelled tarmac track that leads from the road to the camp site. A sign at the side of the tarmac says "NO PARKING PLEASE", and this is a useful marker, for as you go on across the grassy heath you should endeavour to keep the main road about this distance on your right.

You will notice that the railway lurches sharply to the left at this point. This is the first of several twists which earned the line the nickname "Castleman's Corkscrew" when it was built in 1850. Mr Castleman was an influential Victorian environmentalist, and together with his friends he succeeded in saving the old woods around Lyndhurst from destruction by the railway. Enviromental interests in the Forest generally built up following anger at the Deer Removal Act 1851, which included the right to grub-up and enclose vast new acreages; within a few years, centuries of ancient woodland were completely razed. Half the forested area was given up to the Moloch of efficency as orderly rows of pines, occasionally alternated with oaks, were planted out. The deer, however, refused to obey the Act and survived every attempt to remove them. Pressure built up and in 1877 the New Forest Act was passed. This laid the foundations for the modern balance of conservational, farming and tourist interests.

When you reach the next tarmac track you should see a wooden gate marked 'Access Limited' on the other side. If not immediately visible, scout up and down a short way — it is just before a tarmac ramp on the track leading to the main road. Stop at this gate to decide on an option.

Options

a) Take the track straight ahead across the grassy heath — WALK 24A *(50 mins to Lyndhurst, 70 mins to Ashurst).*
b) Turn left up the tarmac track for a wide range of scenic options — WALK 15A *(70 mins to Lyndhurst, 70 mins to Ashurst).*

WALK 26A

This walk is designed in the other direction only.

Walk 27A

Continue up the straight broad track, which shortly becomes bordered with gorse and silver birch again.

This is just a short link track; content yourself in spring with admiring the apple blossom, in summer with anticipating the ripening crop of apples, and in autumn with avoiding the temptation to bite into these horrifically bitter beauties.

After the path narrows, you reach the Lyndhurst to Beaulieu road for your next option point. A much broader track than yours runs off left just before your reach the road.

Options

a) Turn left onto this broad track to pass through Matley Wood — WALK 16 *(80 mins to Lyndhurst, 50 mins to Ashurst).*
b) Turn right for a quick return to Lyndhurst — WALK 28A *(30 mins to Lyndhurst, 60 mins to Ashurst).*
c) Turn left along the road — WALK 22A *(110 mins to Lyndhurst, 100 mins to Ashurst).*

Walk 28A

The walk follows the direction of the road back to Lyndhurst, but fortunately you can avoid being run over by choosing the broad grassy track running a few paces to the right of the road.

Note the dark green Inclosure on your right as you progress. Denny was enclosed in 1870 and this section was planted out with the mentality of the Industrial Age. Scots pines stand in long formal rows, productive of wood, but not much else. There is little chance for beauty or wildlife to flourish where light is too shut out to reach the forest floor. However, we are able to benefit indirectly from this fact on many of our paths, especially on the fringes of Matley Wood ahead — odd little groups of self-sown pines have escaped from the enclosure and established themselves with total disregard to all formality. Thumbing their noses at man's desire for ever more telegraph poles, they have freely taken on some beautiful shapes and forms. At the time this plantation was laid, storms of protest were already rising from locals and visitors alike about the replacement of our Ancient and Ornamental woodlands with rows of boringly uniform sentries. By 1877, a well-meaning Act of Parliment was passed, (still largely the basis of current law), preventing the further enclosing of Forest land. Unfortunately, this law also applies to areas of ancient natural woodland and thus prevents oak and beech seedlings from regenerating naturally, since they are eaten by deer and ponies instead. Ah well, they meant well!

When you reach a group of three birches growing from the same base, you should stop for your next option. You will see the broad ridgeway path curving well away from the road on the right.

Options

a) Follow the road back to Lyndhurst — WALK 23 *(20 mins to Lyndhurst, 85 mins to Ashurst).*
b) Take the ridgeway track — WALK 4A *(25 mins to Lyndhurst, 55 mins to Ashurst).*

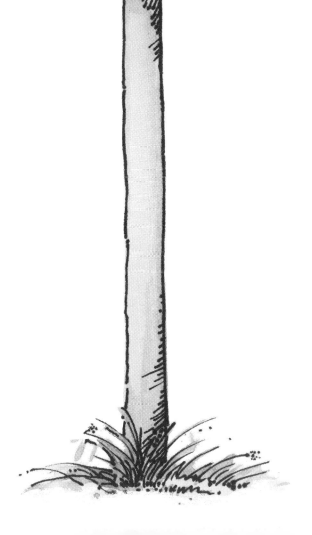

FEEDING OF ANIMALS PROHIBITED PENALTY £20